A DAY IN ANCIENT MAYA

by Janie Havemeyer
illustrated by Cesar Samaniego

Tools for Parents & Teachers

Grasshopper Books enhance imagination and introduce the earliest readers to fun storylines and illustrations. The easy-to-read text supports early reading experiences with repetitive sentence patterns and sight words.

Before Reading

- Discuss the cover illustration. What do readers see?
- Look at the glossary together. Discuss the words.

Read the Book

- Read the book to the child, or have them read independently.
- "Walk" through the book and look at the illustrations. When and where does the story take place? What is happening in the story?

After Reading

- Prompt the child to think more. Ask: What was life like in ancient Maya? What more would you like to learn about this time period?

Grasshopper Books are published by Jump!
5357 Penn Avenue South
Minneapolis, MN 55419
www.jumplibrary.com

Library of Congress Cataloging-in-Publication Data

Names: Havemeyer, Janie, author.
Samaniego, César, 1975- illustrator.
Title: A day in ancient Maya / by Janie Havemeyer; illustrated by Cesar Samaniego
Description: Minneapolis, MN: Jump!, Inc., [2025]
Series: Ancient civilizations | Includes index.
Audience: Ages 7-10
Identifiers: LCCN 2024023356 (print)
LCCN 2024023357 (ebook)
ISBN 9798892134835 (hardcover)
ISBN 9798892134842 (paperback)
ISBN 9798892134859 (ebook)
Subjects: LCSH: Mayas–Social life and customs–Juvenile literature. | Mayas–Civilization–Juvenile literature.
Classification: LCC F1435.3.S7 H38 2025 (print)
LCC F1435.3.S7 (ebook)
DDC 972.81/01–dc23/eng/20240614
LC record available at https://lccn.loc.gov/2024023356
LC ebook record available at https://lccn.loc.gov/2024023357

Editor: Alyssa Sorenson
Direction and Layout: Anna Peterson
Illustrator: Cesar Samaniego
Content Consultant: Edwin Barnhart, PhD, Director of the Maya Exploration Center, Colorado

Printed in the United States of America at Corporate Graphics in North Mankato, Minnesota.

Table of Contents

Work and Play

It is spring in the year 725. The Sun rises over Tikal. It is one of the biggest Maya cities in Central America. A forest surrounds it. Red pyramids rise above the trees.

In the morning, people meet in the city's main **plaza**. They bring goods. A girl trades a clay pot for beads.

5

Across the city, the king places flowers on an altar. He burns **incense**. This **ritual** honors the **gods**. A scribe paints what happens. Why? He **records** the event.

scribe

altar

7

Outside the city, men and boys work in fields. They plant **crops** like corn, beans, and squash.

Women grind corn. They will make it into dough to make **tamales**. They talk and watch their children. One waters plants in a garden. Another feeds turkeys.

9

It gets hotter as the day goes on. A stonecutter shapes a large block of stone. It is for a new pyramid being built in the city. The pyramid will be a **tomb** for the king. Men carry the stone to the city. It will be painted red.

Dancers perform in the plaza. A large crowd watches. They believe dancing creates a stronger connection with the gods. Dancers do the snake dance for Chaac, the god of rain. They hope he is happy and will send rain. The dancers' beaded costumes swish and jingle as they move.

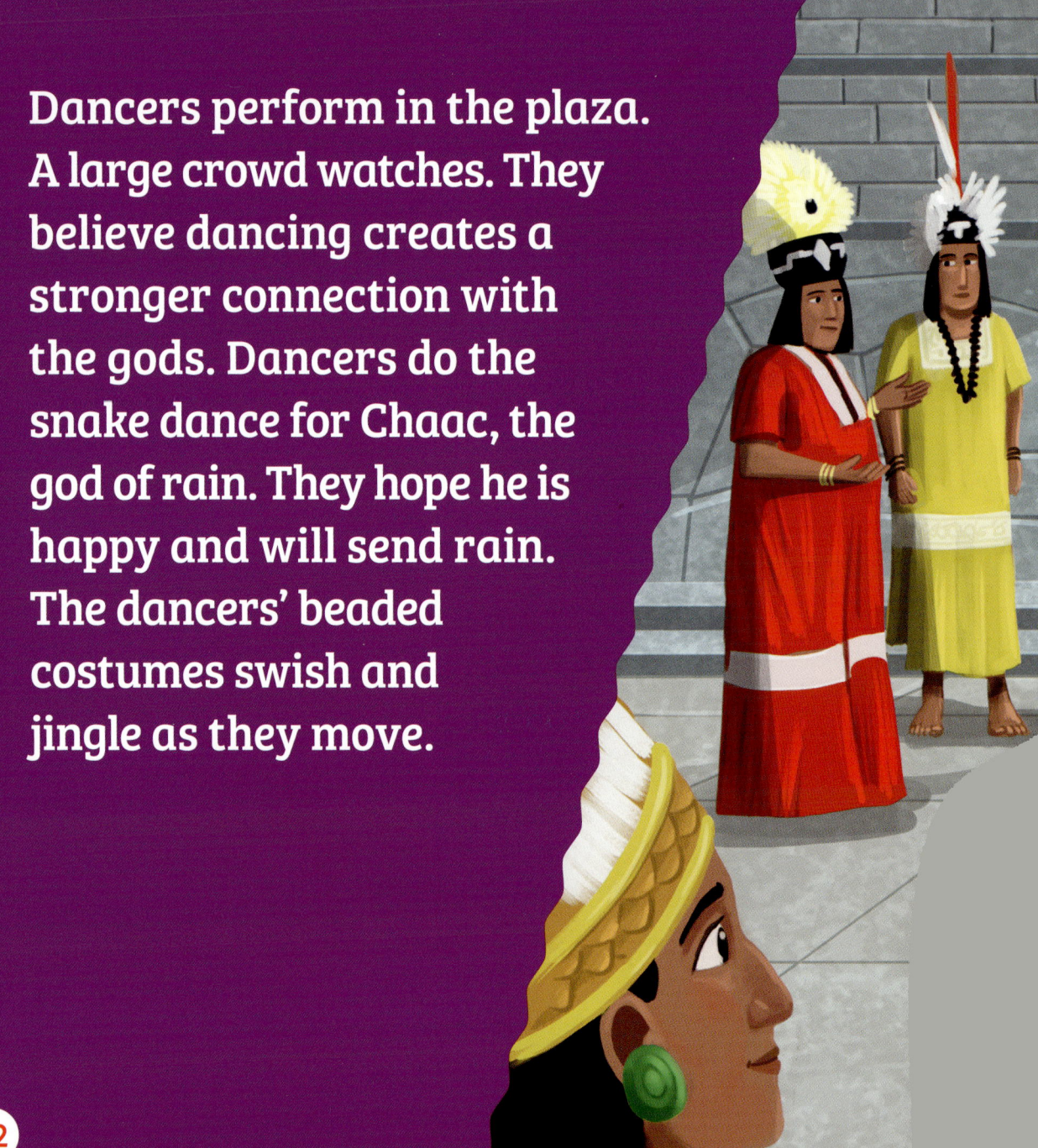

It is time for the big game! Players face off in the ball court. They hit a ball back and forth. They cannot use their hands or feet. They hit the ball with other parts of their bodies instead.

14

One man knocks the ball high in the air. It passes through a stone ring on the court wall. Score!

There is a feast after the game. People gather in the plaza. They cook meat on pit ovens. They eat until they are full.

The king invites **nobles** to his palace to celebrate the game. Musicians pound drums and shake rattles. Guests eat tamales and stew. They drink a spicy, chocolate drink.

19

After the feast, a **priest** climbs to the top of a pyramid. He studies the moon and stars to make a calendar. The Maya use calendars to schedule rituals. They mark important times in ancient Maya!

20

Ancient Maya Timeline

What are some important events in Maya history? Take a look!

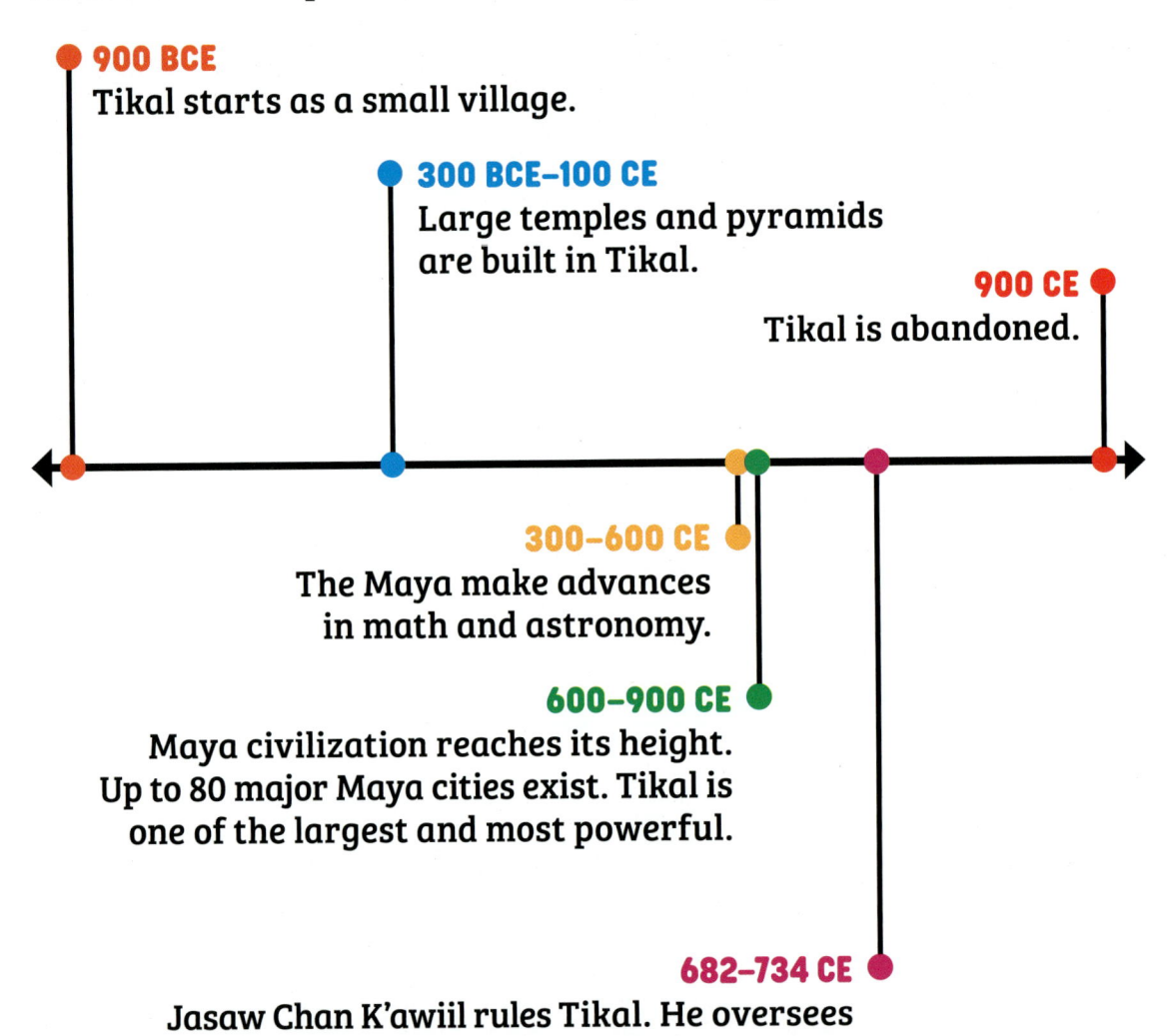

900 BCE
Tikal starts as a small village.

300 BCE–100 CE
Large temples and pyramids are built in Tikal.

900 CE
Tikal is abandoned.

300–600 CE
The Maya make advances in math and astronomy.

600–900 CE
Maya civilization reaches its height. Up to 80 major Maya cities exist. Tikal is one of the largest and most powerful.

682–734 CE
Jasaw Chan K'awiil rules Tikal. He oversees the building of two massive pyramids.

Map of Ancient Maya

Take a look at Maya in 725 CE.

GULF OF
MEXICO

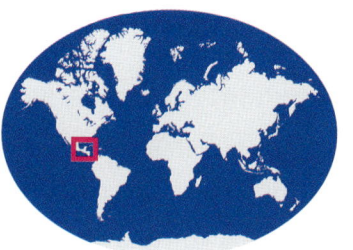

CARIBBEAN
SEA

★
MAYA   Tikal

PACIFIC
OCEAN

N
W ╋ E
S

To Learn More

Finding more information is as easy as 1, 2, 3.

❶ Go to www.factsurfer.com

❷ Enter "**ancientMaya**" into the search box.

❸ Choose your book to see a list of websites.

Glossary

crops: Plants grown for food.

gods: Beings that are worshipped and are believed to have special powers over nature and life.

incense: A substance that burns with a strong, sweet smell and is often used in religious ceremonies.

nobles: People of high social position.

plaza: A wide-open, public square in a city or town.

priest: A religious person who performs rituals and leads prayers.

records: Writes something down so it can be kept.

ritual: A ceremonial action repeated regularly in a certain way.

tamales: A dish of cornmeal dough rolled with meat or beans, wrapped in leaves and steamed.

tomb: A building for holding a dead body.

Index

24